The
Florida
Panther

Other titles in the Returning Wildlife series include:

The Bald Eagle
Bats
Manatees
The North American Beaver
The North American Bison
North American River Otters
Wild Turkeys

Returning Wildlife

The
Florida
Panther

John E. Becker

KIDHAVEN
PRESS™

THOMSON
TM
GALE

San Diego • Detroit • New York • San Francisco • Cleveland
New Haven, Conn. • Waterville, Maine • London • Munich

To Kay and Glenn for their contributions
to wild cat conservation.

For more information, contact
KidHaven Press
27500 Drake Rd.
Farmington Hills, MI 48331-3535
Or you can visit our Internet site at http://www.gale.com

LIBRARY OF CONGRESS CATALOGING-IN-PUBLICATION DATA

Becker, John E., 1942–
The Florida panther / by John E. Becker.
p. cm. — (Returning wildlife)
Includes bibliographical references and index.
Summary: Discusses the physical characteristics and behavior of the species of puma known as the Florida panther, threats to its existence, and efforts to protect these animals.
ISBN 0-7377-1379-8 (hardback : alk. paper)
1. Florida panther—Juvenile literature. [1. Florida panther. 2. Puma. 3. Endangered species.] I. Title. II. Series.
QL737.C23 B36 2004
599.75'24—dc21

                                             2002013944

Printed in the United States of America

Contents

Chapter One 6
    Florida Cougar

Chapter Two 14
    Gradual Disappearance

Chapter Three 22
    Help for Panthers

Chapter Four 32
    Reason for Hope

Glossary 40

For Further Exploration 41

Index 44

Picture Credits 46

Acknowledgments 47

About the Author 48

chapter 1

Florida Cougar

Florida panthers once roamed the American Southeast from Louisiana to the Carolinas and into Florida. Europeans who came to America in the 1500s feared the large, powerful panthers and began hunting them. By the twentieth century, Florida panthers could be found only in remote areas of south Florida.

In the 1970s panthers were given protection as an endangered species. Since that time their numbers have slowly increased thanks to the efforts of dedicated individuals, conservation organizations, and government agencies. Panther numbers remain dangerously low, however.

Ancient Origins

Cats first appeared on Earth more than 30 million years ago. In ancient times there were two branches of the cat family—large saber-toothed cats known as **nimravids** and smaller, quicker cats known as **felids**. About ten thousand years ago the nimravids disappeared, but the felids continued to flourish. Today, felids can be found on every continent except Australia and Antarctica. They have remained almost unchanged for 10 million years.

One of the most successful and wide-ranging felid species is the cougar. Cougars have lived in the Americas for more than 5 million years. When the first Europeans arrived in the New World, cougars ranged from the Arctic Circle in the north to the tip of South America. They have survived through the centuries because of their success as skillful hunters.

People have given cougars many names, including puma, painter, catamount, mountain lion, and panther. Recently, the scientific name for cougars was changed to *Puma concolor* (one color). The scientific name for a Florida panther is *Puma concolor coryi*.

Perfect Predators

Like other cats, panthers are skilled climbers. They can easily follow a prey animal up a tree, or take cover in a tree if being chased. Panthers prefer to stay on the ground, however.

The cougar's muscular legs and long stride make it a fast runner and deadly hunter.

Panthers are very **territorial** and mark the boundaries of their hunting territory with scrapes of soil, leaves, pine needles, and scent markings. Other panthers easily find these signs.

As large **carnivores**, Florida panthers are at the top of the food chain. Panthers usually hunt alone and are most active at night. During the heat of the day, panthers generally rest in the shade.

Panthers are built for springing onto prey animals, but panthers are also capable of running at fast speeds for a short distance. The panther's long, muscular legs and flexible spine allow it to take long strides. A long tail gives a panther the balance it needs to turn quickly in a chase.

Panthers usually eat white-tailed deer, hogs, raccoons, or armadillos. If those animals are not available, panthers will also eat birds, rabbits, rats, and alligators.

Panthers need to eat quite often if their prey is small. If the prey is large, such as a deer or hog, the panther may feed on the kill, off and on, for a week. After the panther has eaten its fill, it will scrape leaves, twigs, and pine needles over the carcass to hide it. When the panther is hungry again it will return and feed on the **cache** for several days. A mother panther with kittens will cover the carcass and return with the kittens so they may also eat.

Sharp Claws and Keen Senses

Like other cats, Florida panthers have razor-sharp claws that retract into their paws when not in use. Sharp claws allow panthers to capture their prey and hold on while they apply a killing bite with sharp, powerful teeth. Pound for pound, wild cats are some of the strongest animals on Earth. A panther is usually successful in overpowering an animal and killing it. Panthers eat between twenty and thirty pounds of meat at a time (equal to 80 to 120 quarter-pound hamburgers). Females with nursing kittens may even eat more.

A hungry panther uses its sharp teeth to rip the flesh from a freshly killed deer.

A prowling panther uses its keen senses to detect prey and danger.

Panthers have very good eyesight. Their eyes are larger than those of other carnivores and are especially good for hunting at night. A reflective coating on the back of a cat's eyes known as **tapetum lucidum** makes its eyes glow at night. The tapetum lucidum also allows cats to see much better at night than humans can because light is reflected from one part of the cat's eye to another.

Panthers also hear very well. A panther has the ability to move its ears to pick up sounds coming from different directions. It can hear sounds in an **ultrasonic** range that people cannot hear. The high-pitched sounds made by a mouse, for example, help a panther locate it in much the same way that an owl locates a mouse.

The panther's other senses, such as smell, are also well developed. Those senses do not play as important a role in hunting as sight and hearing do, however.

Panthers are generally quiet, but they can communicate with sounds. Kittens will make a series of high-pitched peeps when frightened. A kitten and its mother keep in contact with each other with whistles. Other panther sounds include growls, hisses, purrs, chirps, and screams. When females are ready to mate, they tell males by **yowling** or **caterwauling**.

Reproduction

Panthers live alone for most of their lives after leaving their mothers at about two years of age. Male and female panthers will stay together for up to a week, however, during mating.

Three months after a female panther becomes pregnant, she will give birth to a litter of one to four kittens. Kittens can be born anytime throughout the year, but most are born in late spring.

A panther kitten weighs about a pound when born. Its eyes and ears are closed and it has black spots in its grayish brown coat. Its eyes and ears open, and it can walk by two to three weeks of age. Panther kittens' eyes are blue.

A mother panther raises her young alone. Kittens begin to follow their mother on hunts at about two months of age. They begin hunting on their own by nine to twelve months and catch small prey. By a year and a half they will begin to hunt deer and hogs.

Unfortunately, panthers do not live very long. Female panthers may live ten to fifteen years in the wild. Males, on the other hand, frequently die before reaching six, due to deadly encounters with older males.

Special Characteristics

Compared to other North American cougars, Florida panthers are smaller, and have longer legs and smaller feet. Male panthers weigh between 100 and 150 pounds (the same as a Great Dane dog), while a male western cougar may weigh as much as 200 pounds. Female panthers are smaller than males and weigh between 65 and 100 pounds. A panther will generally be six to seven feet long from its nose to the tip of its tail. Cougars may grow to more than eight feet long. Florida panthers are usually more reddish brown in color than other cougars. The fur on a panther is also shorter in length.

For many years scientists thought that panthers had some characteristics not found in other cougars. For example, characteristics on the panther's back, such as a

This blue-eyed panther cub takes its first steps, careful not to wander out of its mother's reach.

A thirsty panther cautiously approaches a pond for a drink of water.

cowlick, or a patch of hair growing in the opposite direction as the rest of the hair; a right-angle kink in the panther's tail; and white flecks around the panther's neck were believed to be unique to panthers.

Scientists now believe that the cowlick and tail kink are characteristics resulting from **inbreeding** (when closely related animals breed with each other). The white flecks are believed to be the result of tick bites.

Habitat

Like all living creatures, Florida panthers need habitat that provides food, water, and shelter. Panthers prefer to live in forested areas, but prairies, marshes, and swamps are also part of their territory in southwest Florida. Unfortunately, growing human populations in Florida have made habitat loss one of the main threats to panthers.

chapter 2

Gradual Disappearance

For thousands of years Florida panthers and Native Americans lived in the same territory with little difficulty. But when Europeans settled in North America they viewed panthers as a danger to themselves and to their livestock. As a result of that threat panthers began to disappear because white settlers killed them at every opportunity. One of the main causes for the disappearance of panthers has been hunting.

People Hunting Panthers

Panthers' main prey is deer. For centuries, land in Florida was sparsely populated and deer were plentiful. But that began to change when whites settled those areas in the 1500s. White settlers killed deer for themselves and also traded with Indian tribes for deer hides. That trade helped to reduce the panthers' main food source. In only one year, 1771, more than 250,000 pounds of deer hides were shipped to England. Each hide weighed a pound and a half. This means that more than 165,000 deer were killed. Still, panthers were not in trouble as a species until the 1800s.

It was not until Florida became a territory of the United States in 1821, however, that panther numbers began to be reduced in Florida. The United States encouraged settlement in the new territory, and the promise of land attracted settlers. The first census in Florida in 1830 showed that approximately thirty-five thousand people lived in the territory at that time.

As settlers established farms and ranches, they wanted to eliminate panthers to protect their livestock. One method was to offer a **bounty**, or reward, for killing panthers. The success of that effort could be seen in 1874 when a British visitor to Florida noted that panthers were becoming scarce. In 1887 the state of Florida offered five dollars for panther scalps, and "sport" hunting of panthers further reduced their numbers.

Early Florida settlers get ready for a deer hunt in this painting.

Beginning in 1939 the panther population became even smaller. People in Florida believed that a tick carried by deer caused a disease outbreak in domestic cattle. Between 1939 and 1941 ten thousand deer were destroyed by hunters hired by the state of Florida. The loss of so much of the panthers' main food source caused panther numbers to decline because underfed females generally have fewer kittens, and the surviving kittens may have starved.

Ranchers continued to kill panthers because they believed that panthers kill cattle. This further endangered panthers, even though research showed that panthers rarely kill cattle.

Deer are a major source of food for the Florida panther.

The legal hunting of panthers continued into the late 1950s, however, when another threat posed an even greater danger to panthers.

Rapid Human Population Growth in Florida

Millions of people moved to Florida during the last half of the twentieth century. In 1950, approximately 3 million lived in Florida. In 2000, almost 16 million did. That rate of growth created a number of problems for Florida panthers and other wildlife. The few panthers surviving at that time were forced to live in smaller areas as humans destroyed their habitat. In the 1960s land near Naples was subdivided and canals were dug for a huge housing development. As the urban areas continued to grow, more and more panther habitat was turned into housing developments, golf courses, and businesses. Between 1936 and 1987 one-third of all forested land in south Florida was lost to human development.

Many new roads were also constructed during the last half of the twentieth century to carry an ever-increasing number of cars across Florida. As the number of vehicles steadily grew, panthers were hit while crossing highways. One roadway in particular, Alligator Alley, from Fort Lauderdale to Naples, became a dangerous crossing for panthers. From the time Alligator Alley was completed in 1968, more panthers have died on that stretch of highway than on any other highway in Florida.

The panther population suffered another setback when, in the late 1960s, heavy rainfall and water pumped from flooded farmlands to the Everglades in south Florida caused thousands of deer to drown. Thereafter, an already low panther population dropped to extremely low numbers.

During the late twentieth century, pollution of air, land, and water also harmed Florida. The water that panthers drink and the air they breathe contain chemicals that are dangerous to living creatures. Just how many health problems those chemicals have caused for panthers is the subject of much debate. After one female panther died, a medical examination showed that she had an extremely high level of mercury in her system. Mercury is an element found in water polluted from industrial waste and can be deadly to wildlife. Because no other dead panthers have been found with high levels of deadly chemicals in their systems, the exact dangers of pollution are still unknown. Some scientists continue to believe, however, that dangerous chemicals may prevent panthers from having healthy kittens.

Reintroduction and Captive-Breeding Experiments

In 1987 a plan was developed to establish two additional populations of panthers in areas outside of south Florida. The following spring five Texas cougars were flown to Florida. They were fitted with **radio collars** and released into the wild in north Florida near the Osceola National Forest. Unfortunately, problems developed shortly after the release. Four of the cougars died, including two that were shot illegally.

Two more cougars from Texas were released in the same area in March 1989. Thereafter, the cougars wandered into urban areas and became a problem by killing livestock. Therefore, all the cats were recaptured in May 1989.

A second part of the reintroduction project called for taking Florida panther kittens from the wild and raising them in captivity. Later, their offspring would be released into their natural habitat. That **captive-breeding pro-**

gram began in 1991 with six kittens taken from the wild and placed at White Oak Plantation near Jacksonville. Four more kittens were removed from the wild and joined the others at White Oak in 1992. Before these animals were allowed to breed, however, concerns about inbreeding problems, such as heart damage and **infertility**, caused wildlife officials to stop the project. Unfortunately, ten years passed before those panthers were given the opportunity to breed. By that time they were beyond their ideal breeding age, and none of the female panthers has given birth to kittens.

From 1993 to 1995 a second group of Texas cougars was released in north Florida. Nineteen cougars, eleven

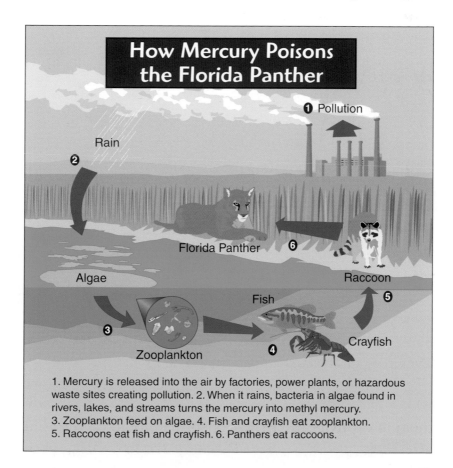

How Mercury Poisons the Florida Panther

1. Mercury is released into the air by factories, power plants, or hazardous waste sites creating pollution. 2. When it rains, bacteria in algae found in rivers, lakes, and streams turns the mercury into methyl mercury.
3. Zooplankton feed on algae. 4. Fish and crayfish eat zooplankton.
5. Raccoons eat fish and crayfish. 6. Panthers eat raccoons.

A captive-bred panther peers out from behind the bars of its enclosure.

females and eight males, were radio-collared and set free. That group had a much greater survival rate than those released in 1988 and 1989. Researchers were pleased that the study showed that panthers could survive in areas outside of south Florida. Some people strongly opposed the project because of possible human-panther conflicts. Scientists hope, however, that two additional sites will be found to provide permanent new homes for panthers. In 2002 the total adult Florida panther population was estimated at fewer than eighty.

chapter 3

Help for Panthers

The air was filled with the sound of dogs barking and footsteps crashing through the leafy underbrush. The barking became louder and the sound of a cat hissing and spitting added to the noise. When the tracker caught up to his dogs, he could see the Florida panther sitting in a tree growling at the dogs below.

Moments later, a capture team from the Florida Fish and Wildlife Conservation Commission (FWC) arrived. The team included a veterinarian and two wildlife biologists.

The veterinarian quickly loaded a tranquilizer dart into a rifle and handed the rifle to the tracker. The other team members inflated an air mattress, and then spread a large net on the ground. The tracker, taking steady aim at the panther, slowly squeezed the trigger.

Foomp! The sound of the rifle was followed by a loud hiss from the panther as the dart hit its mark. After several minutes the panther's eyes closed. Then it fell out of the tree onto the air mattress below.

The medical team immediately began checking the panther for parasites, taking blood samples, making measurements, and weighing the panther. Then the panther was given shots to prevent diseases.

After the medical examination was completed, the cat was fitted with a radio collar. The collar allowed scientists to track the cat to see where it would go and what type of habitat it liked. The panther is now, officially, part of the Florida Panther Recovery Program.

A wide-eyed panther perches on a tree branch and watches the ground below.

Early Efforts to Halt the Decline of Panthers

In 1947 President Harry S. Truman dedicated 1.3 million acres in south Florida as Everglades National Park (ENP). That huge tract of land was made a park to protect the native plant and animal species of that region of Florida. ENP also became a sanctuary for panthers and has played an important role in their survival.

Park rangers take a blood sample from a tranquilized panther.

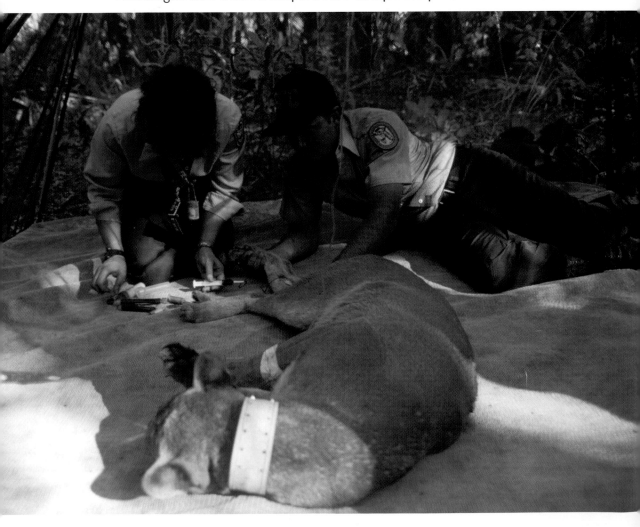

Panthers were further helped in the 1940s and 1950s when white-tailed deer were released for hunters in south Florida, and when laws were passed in Florida to protect panthers. When the state declared panthers an endangered species in 1958, it marked the first significant effort to ensure that panthers would not disappear.

Beginning in 1961 and continuing for sixteen years, the Florida Game and Freshwater Fish Commission released thousands of wild hogs in the Big Cypress Swamp area. The hogs were also released for hunters, but they provided another important source of food for panthers.

More Protection

The federal government gave protection to Florida panthers and other endangered species in 1973 when Congress passed the Endangered Species Act (ESA). The federal agency charged with the responsibility of restoring panthers, and other endangered wildlife, under the ESA is the U.S. Fish and Wildlife Service (FWS). FWS enforces the ESA by outlawing the killing, harming, or trading of Florida panthers. FWS is also responsible for protecting panther habitat, and for buying land needed for the survival of panthers. A recovery plan for returning panthers to healthy population levels was also required under the ESA. A recovery team made up of experts from government agencies and private conservation organizations oversees the recovery plan.

One important part of the recovery plan is the purchase of land for the protection of panthers. In 1974 the federal government established Big Cypress National Preserve (BCNP) located west of ENP in south Florida. In that same year the state of Florida also established the Fakahatchee Strand State Preserve west of BCNP. The Florida Panther National Wildlife Refuge was set aside as a federal

This panther's radio collar will help scientists monitor the cat's activities in the wild.

preserve in 1989. That 26,400-acre site was the first sanctuary of its kind reserved for panther preservation by the federal government.

The state agency primarily responsible for protecting panthers is the FWC. FWC enforces state laws protecting panthers and their habitat, and it leads state efforts to help panthers recover. FWC biologists are responsible for capturing, radio-collaring, and following panthers in the wild.

Conservation Strategy for Panthers

In 1976 representatives from government agencies and private organizations met for the first time to discuss ways in which panthers could be preserved. Because panthers are solitary and secretive, some people questioned whether any panthers still existed in Florida at that time.

Two years passed before evidence of a surviving panther population could be found. Unfortunately, the proof came when a panther was illegally shot. This led the state of Florida to raise the penalty for killing panthers from a misdemeanor (minor crime) to a felony (major crime).

The swampy Big Cypress National Preserve provides a safe home for panthers.

After that, researchers made a thorough search for panthers in south Florida. Their efforts were rewarded when they found the tracks of five Florida panthers in BCNP.

Scientists and researchers are not the only ones to become involved in the panther cause. In 1982 Florida schoolchildren chose the panther as the official state animal of Florida. That project also helped to focus attention on and raise awareness of the plight of panthers.

Private Organizations

Private organizations also play an important role in the conservation of Florida panthers. In 1994 the Florida Panther Society (FPS) was founded to voice community support for panther recovery programs. FPS works with agencies, other environmental groups, and the public. It

A researcher examines an injured panther that was hit by a car.

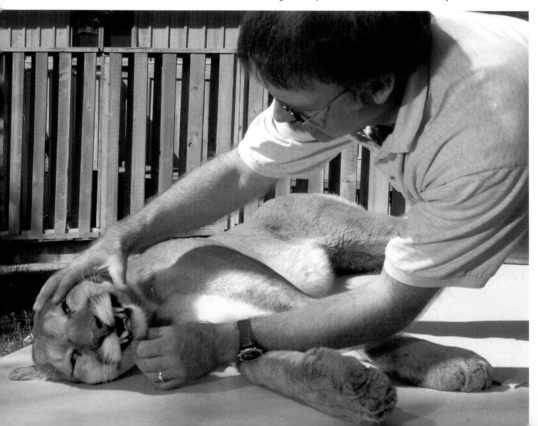

A young girl feeds a five-day-old panther cub at a Florida refuge.

distributes educational information about panthers and coordinates meetings, conferences, and workshops.

Defenders of Wildlife is a conservation organization focused on protecting endangered plants and animals and preventing habitat destruction. Defenders takes an active role in reducing habitat loss in south Florida, and it encourages the protecting of land for a growing panther population. Defenders also promote the building of highway

A "Panther Crossing" sign warns drivers to watch out for panthers crossing the highway.

underpasses such as those included in the construction of a modern superhighway to replace the deadly Alligator Alley, which has claimed so many panthers' lives. The new highway, I-75, was built with a ten-foot-high fence along the highway and underpasses below the highway. Those protective measures greatly increased the cost of the project, but it helped to protect panthers from collisions with cars and trucks.

After seven panthers were killed on other highways in the spring of 2001, Defenders joined with FWC to increase public awareness of the danger of panthers crossing roads. Defenders has encouraged local governments to add signs about panthers crossing roadways, and it has encouraged the lowering of speed limits in panther-crossing areas. Defenders has also joined with other organizations to prevent building projects in important panther habitat areas.

Some people are helping Florida panthers by joining organizations such as Friends of the Florida Panther Refuge. Friends educates people about Florida panthers, raises money for panther-related projects, and provides volunteers for the refuge. Friends has also helped in the development of a trail through a portion of the refuge. Friends, in partnership with the Wings of Hope "Pennies for Panthers" project of Florida Gulf Coast University (FGCU), raised money to help purchase an infrared camera that refuge biologists use to track panthers.

Another Friends and FGCU program allows fourth-grade students to learn how radio collars work. Through the program radio-collared panthers are monitored in the schools. This gives children a realistic view of panther research in action. Students also create a bulletin board about panthers, and they learn how to recognize panther paw prints. Students in schools across the United States can participate in the program through the Friends' website.

Zoos have also contributed to Florida panther conservation. Lowry Park Zoo in Tampa, for example, has maintained captive panthers for many years. This has given scientists an opportunity to learn about panthers from direct observations. Information gathered at the zoo has been used in developing strategies to help restore panthers.

A Long Way to Go

A great deal of effort has gone into protecting panthers, but much more remains to be done. There is every reason to believe that human populations will continue to grow in Florida. If that growth continues to take away panther habitat, panthers will disappear.

chapter 4

Reason for Hope

The early morning sun flickered through the trees as the wildlife biologist climbed into the huge swamp buggy. The biologist had traveled only a short distance through the Florida Panther National Wildlife Refuge when he brought the swamp buggy to a halt. He jumped down and looked at a scrape made by a panther. The scrape tells other panthers that the territory is taken.

Nearby, the biologist noticed a fresh paw print. He knelt down to have a closer look.

"That looks like number fifty-nine," he said to himself.

He went back to the swamp buggy and brought out a radio receiver, which looked like an old-fashioned television antenna. He listened to the radio receiver until he heard, "*Beep, beep, beep.*"

"Good!" he exclaimed. "Number fifty-nine is still within his territory and moving normally."

The above scene is acted out on a regular basis wherever panthers roam in southwest Florida. With fewer than eighty adult panthers, it is very important that wildlife biologists continue to keep track of the panthers' movements.

Three days a week FWC biologists also fly in small planes to check on the movements of radio-collared panthers. By carrying out these **aerial surveys** biologists collect important information about panthers, their movements, and their behaviors. The information gathered is of great value in developing strategies to save panthers from extinction. These aerial surveys will continue to be an important part of Florida panther conservation well into the future.

Problems Remain

It is estimated that more than 20 million people will live in Florida by the year 2015. As Florida's human population grows, more land will be needed to meet the needs of those people. Loss of habitat, therefore, continues to be the single greatest threat to panthers today, and each year panther habitat decreases.

A panther marks its territory by clawing a tree trunk. Habitat loss is a serious threat to panthers.

As panther habitat is reduced, the number of deadly conflicts among panthers increases. Panthers are territorial, especially males. When greater numbers of male panthers are forced to live in smaller land areas, they come in contact more often. Fatal injuries from panthers fighting with each other have become the most common cause of panther deaths over the past several years. Those deaths are usually the result of a smaller, younger male trespassing on a larger, older male's territory. Occasionally, however, male panthers will also kill a female's kittens, thus reducing future competition for food and territory.

Collisions with cars and trucks will undoubtedly continue to affect the panther population as more and more vehicles cross roadways in panther habitat. The number of vehicles in Florida has grown steadily as the number of people has increased. Over the past several years, there has been an alarming increase in the number of panthers killed on the highways of south Florida. Forty-six panthers have been killed on Florida highways since 1972.

Continuing Projects

One extremely important objective of the Florida Panther Recovery Plan is to establish additional populations of panthers outside of south Florida. The reintroduction studies carried out in north Florida in 1988 and 1989 and from 1993 through 1995 proved that it is possible for panthers to survive in areas other than their historic range. Fourteen sites throughout the southeastern United States have been chosen as release sites for Florida panthers. Some scientists believe that it is extremely important for panther survival to establish two additional populations of panthers outside of south Florida in the very near future.

When Alligator Alley was replaced by Interstate 75 in 1993, thirty-six underpasses were built at various places

This panther defends its territory by snarling aggressively at intruders.

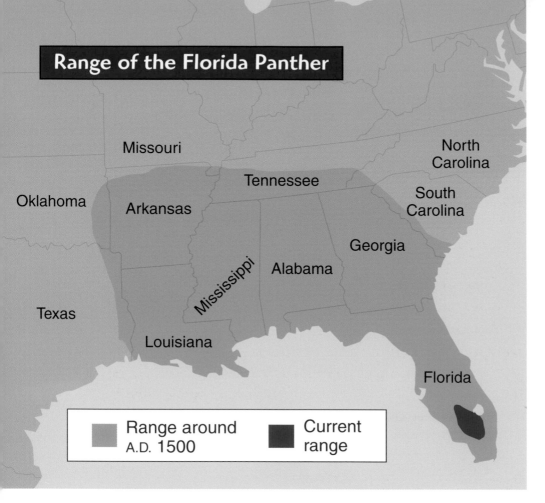

Range of the Florida Panther

Missouri

North Carolina

Tennessee

Oklahoma

Arkansas

South Carolina

Georgia

Mississippi   Alabama

Texas

Louisiana

Florida

Range around
A.D. 1500

Current
range

along the route. Those underpasses, known as wildlife crossings, allow panthers and other animals to cross from one side to the other without going on the highway. Since the wildlife crossings were constructed, not a single panther has been hit by a vehicle near the crossings. The success of these underpasses has led to wildlife crossings being built under other highways that go through panther habitat. In 2002 forty-one wildlife crossings existed under roadways in south Florida, and several more are planned for the future.

Another effort to save panthers is a controversial plan to increase their **genetic diversity**. In 1995 eight female Texas cougars were released in south Florida in hopes that they would breed with male Florida panthers. The female cougars and male panthers did breed, and several litters of kittens were born. By 2002 seventeen kittens had been born and twelve of these were still alive. The project has been successful in introducing new genes to the panther population. Some scientists are concerned, however, that Texas cougar genes may become too numerous. Those scientists urge caution in relying on Texas cougars alone to increase panther populations. They recommend reintroducing panthers into north Florida, and beginning another captive-breeding program.

One of the most important conservation strategies for panthers is the purchase of land for panther sanctuaries. In recent years thousands of acres of land have been purchased by both the state of Florida and by the federal government. Two important purchases were the Picayune Strand State Forest, which was established in 1996, and the additional land that was purchased to increase the size of Big Cypress National Preserve in 1998.

People Helping Panthers

In an effort to raise money for panther conservation, the state of Florida began issuing special panther license plates in 1993. Since the beginning of that program, the license plates have raised more than $35 million. That money pays for panther projects sponsored by the state of Florida.

One way that children are helping panthers is through a project coordinated by the National Wildlife Federation and U.S. Department of Agriculture. The goal of the program is to eliminate an Australian tree that is seriously damaging panther habitat. Australian melaleuca trees were brought to Florida years ago to dry out wetland areas by absorbing water at an extremely rapid rate. Unfortunately, much of south Florida is now overly dry and the melaleuca

Panther populations continue to grow with the help of captive breeding programs.

A panther investigates a fallen tree stump.

trees are a threat to the delicate balance of nature. These trees are spreading at the rate of 11 acres a day. (More than 250,000 acres of land are now covered by these trees.) To stop the spread of the melaleuca trees, Lee County Scouts, Pack Eleven, helped scientists release melaleuca leaf weevils that were imported from Australia. The weevils, with the help of scouts, will help to reduce the threat of melaleuca trees in panther habitat.

A Hopeful Outlook

With less than eighty adult Florida panthers living today, the survival of panthers is not assured. But with increased land set aside for their protection, and additional populations of panthers outside of south Florida, panthers may yet survive into the future.

aerial survey: A view from the air of the movements of animals.

bounty: A reward given for the killing of an animal.

cache: A hiding place for food.

captive-breeding program: Breeding animals in a captive environment such as a zoo or preserve.

carnivores: Animals that eat meat.

caterwauling: Making a long, wailing cry.

felids: Ancient cats that have survived to today.

genetic diversity: Genes from a wide range of donors.

inbreeding: Breeding with closely related family members.

infertility: Being unable to have offspring.

nimravids: Extinct type of cats characterized by large saberlike teeth.

radio collars: Electronic devices that send out radio signals used to track animals.

tapetum lucidum: Reflective coating on the inner surface of a cat's eye.

territorial: Protective of a particular area.

ultrasonic: Sounds that are too high in frequency for human ears to hear.

yowling: Making a long, distressful cry.

Books

Jalma Barrett, *Cougar.* Woodbridge, CT: Blackbirch Press, 1999. Examines the social life of the cougar, the habitat it lives in, its physical characteristics, and its encounters with humans.

Margaret Goff Clark, *The Endangered Florida Panther.* New York: Cobblehill Books, 1993. Presents the story of efforts to save the endangered Florida panther from extinction, as well as information about panthers' physical characteristics, behaviors, and habitat.

Alvin and Virginia Silverstein and Laura Silverstein Nunn, *The Florida Panther.* Brookfield, CT: Millbrook Press, 1997. Details the complex problem of coordinating governmental agencies, conservation organizations, and private citizens in a unified effort to save Florida panthers from extinction.

Periodicals

Mark Jerome Walters, "Gone with the Wind?" *Animals,* January/February 1998.

U.S. Kids, "The Cry of a Ghost," April/May 1999.

Organizations to Contact

The Florida Panther Society, Inc.
Rt. 1, Box 1895
White Springs, FL 32096
386-397-2945
www.atlantic.net

This organization coordinates public support of conservation activities for Florida panthers through educational programs.

Defenders of Wildlife
National Headquarters
1101 14th St., NW, #1400
Washington, DC 20005
202-682-9400
www.defenders.org

An organization dedicated to the conservation of all native wild animals and plants.

The International Society for Endangered Cats
3070 Riverside Dr., Suite 160
Columbus, OH 43221
614-487-8760
www.isec.org

An organization focused on preserving the thirty-six species of wild cats worldwide.

Websites

Florida Fish and Wildlife Conservation Commission—Florida Panther Net (www.panther.state.fl.us). This outstanding site presents abundant information about Florida panthers including physical characteristics, behaviors, threats to their survival, habitat needs, and conservation activities for their recovery. The site also presents a timeline of historic developments through the centuries relating to Florida panthers.

Friends of the Florida Panther Refuge (www.florida panther.org). This site provides information about the activities of the Friends group in support of the U.S. Fish and Wildlife Service's Florida Panther National Wildlife Refuge.

National Wildlife Federation—Florida Panther—Keep the Wild Alive Campaign (www.nwf.org). This site provides extensive information about Florida panthers, including scientific facts about this cougar subspecies, how people can help save panthers, and the efforts of the National Wildlife Federation to preserve panthers and their habitat.

Video

Audubon's Animal Adventures: Panther & Cougar Adventures: HBO Kids Video: National Audubon Society, 1997. A family video about cougars, their physical characteristics, behaviors, and geographic range. The video also includes basic information about the endangered Florida panther.

Index

aerial surveys, 32
Alligator Alley, 17, 30, 34

Big Cypress National Preserve
  (BCNP), 25, 37
Boy Scouts, 39

caches, 8
captive-breeding programs, 18,
  37
claws, 8
climbers, 7
coloration, 12
communication, 11
conservation
  captive-breeding programs
    and, 18, 37
  education and, 28, 31
  Endangered Species Act and,
    25
  Florida Fish and Wildlife Con-
    servation Commission and,
    22, 26, 32
  genetic diversity breeding pro-
    gram and, 36–37
  money for, 37
  private organizations and,
    28–31, 37, 39
  reintroduction and, 18–19, 21,
    34
  sanctuaries and, 24, 25–26, 37
  U.S. Department of Agriculture
    and, 37
  U.S. Fish and Wildlife Service
    and, 25
  wildlife crossings and, 36
  zoos and, 31
cougars, 6–7

deer
  humans and, 14, 16
  loss of, 17
  reintroduction of, 25
Defenders of Wildlife, 29–31
diseases, 22

education, 28, 31
endangered species, 6, 25
Endangered Species Act (ESA),
  25
Everglades National Park (ENP),
  24
eyes, 9

Fakahatchee Strand State Pre-
  serve, 25
felids, 6
Florida
  growth of, 17
  settlement of, 14–15
Florida Fish and Wildlife Conser-
  vation Commission (FWC), 22,
  26, 32
Florida Gulf Coast University
  (FGCU), 31
Florida Panther National Wildlife
  Refuge, 25–26
Florida Panther Recovery Pro-
  gram, 22
Floida panthers
  characteristics of, 8, 12–13, 27
Florida Panther Society (FPS), 28
Friends of the Florida Panther
  Refuge, 31
fur, 12

genetic diversity breeding program, 36–37

habitat
  described, 13
  loss of, 13, 14, 17, 33–34
  see also names of specific
    parks
hearing, sense of, 9
highways, 17, 30–31, 34, 36
hogs, 25
humans
  habitat loss and, 13, 14, 17, 33
  hunting by, 15, 16–17, 21, 27
  pollution and, 18

hunting
  by panthers
    body and, 8
    climbing and, 7
  by kittens, 11
  nocturnal, 8
  senses and, 9
  speed and, 8

inbreeding, 13
Interstate 75, 30, 34, 36

kittens
  at birth, 11
  captive-breeding programs
    and, 18
  communication by, 11
  feeding of, 8
  hunting by, 11
  as prey, 34
  survival of, 16

Lee County Scouts, Pack Eleven,
  39
legs, 8
license plates, 37
life spans, 11
litters, 11, 16
Lowry Zoo Park, 31

mating, 11, 13
melaleuca trees, 37, 39
mercury, 18

National Wildlife Federation, 37
nimravids, 6

origins, 6

"Pennies for Panthers," 31
Picayune Strand State Forest, 37
pollution, 18
population, 18
prey

amount needed, 8
  kittens as, 34
  of panthers, 8, 14, 17, 21, 25
  panthers as, 15, 16–17, 21, 27
Puma concolor, 7
Puma concolor coryi, 7

radio collars, 18, 22, 31
rainfall, 17
range, 6
reintroduction, 18–19, 21, 34
reproduction, 11, 13, 16

sanctuaries. *see names of
  specific parks*
sight, sense of, 9
size, 11–12
speed, 8
spine, 8
strength, 8

tail, 8
tapetum lucidum, 9
territory
  fighting over, 34
  marking of, 8, 32
ticks, 16
Truman, Harry S., 24

U.S. Department of Agriculture
  (USDA), 37
U.S. Fish and Wildlife Service
  (FWS), 25

vision, 9

weather, 17
weight, 11–12
White Oak Plantation, 19
wildlife crossings, 36
Wings of Hope. *See* "Pennies for
  Panthers"

zoos, 31

Acknowledgments

Virginia Edmonds, Lowry Park Zoo
Karen C. Hill, Florida Panther Society
E. Darrell Land, Florida Fish and Wildlife
Conservation Commission
Mark Lotz, Florida Fish and Wildlife
Conservation Commission
David S. Maehr, University of Kentucky
Larry W. Richardson, U.S. Fish and Wildlife Service
Jake Scott, National Wildlife Federation
Trisha White, Defenders of Wildlife

Dr. John E. Becker writes books and magazine articles about nature and wild animals for children. He graduated from Ohio State University in the field of education. He has been an elementary school teacher, college professor, and zoo administrator. Dr. Becker has also worked in the field of wildlife conservation with the International Society for Endangered Cats. He currently lives in Delaware, Ohio, and teaches writing at the Thurber Writing Academy. He also enjoys visiting schools and sharing his love of writing with kids. In his spare time, Dr. Becker likes to read, hike in the woods, ice skate, and play tennis.